OUR PROPHET

MUHAMMAD, RASULULLAH
Salla Allahu 'Alaihi wa Sallam

WORKBOOK

ELEMENTARY LEVEL — PART II

IQRA' PROGRAM OF SÎRAH

Part of

*A Comprehensive and Systematic Program of
Islamic Studies*

Bushra Yasmin Ghazi

IQRA' INTERNATIONAL EDUCATIONAL FOUNDATION
Chicago

Part of a Comprehensive and Systematic Program of Islamic Studies

A Workbook for
the Program of Sirah
Elementary Level

Our Prophet Workbook: Part Two

Chief Program Editors
Dr. Abidullah al-Ansari Ghazi
Ph.D., Harvard University

Tasneema Khatoon Ghazi
Ph.D., University of Minnesota

Religious Review
Rabita al-Alam al-Islami
Makkah Mukarramah

Library of Congress Control Number: Pending
ISBN # 1-56316-153-2

ACKNOWLEDGEMENTS

All praises are due to Allah, the Beneficient, the Merciful.

The *Sîrah* project began when I was thirteen and tearfully left my home in Minneapolis for a new life in Chicago, despite my parents' assurances that "Allah knows best." Allah did know best. Over the last five years I have had the double pleasure of watching the project grow and participating in it myself; initially, as the subject of field-tests; then, as artist and language editor; and, with the publication of this workbook, as an author.

I am grateful for the love and support of Rashid, Saba, Suhaib, and Usama, who never tired of threatening to shake my pen just as I completed a final drawing, my father, who trusted me with this task and guided it to completion, and my mother, who put up with my graphic materials all over the dining room table for three years. Our work on the *Sîrah* has strengthened our bonds as a family.

I am also indebted to my brothers and sisters at the M.C.C. School of Islamic Studies, especially the youth who befriended me and my energetic second grade students who proved to me the need for these books.

Dr. Abdullah Omar Naseef, President of King Abdulaziz University, has supported our project since its inception. The publication of this workbook would not have been possible without his commitment.

Finally, special and sincere thanks go to my friends and teachers at North Shore Country Day for accepting, understanding and challenging me. My four years at North Shore were unique educational experience, one I shall never forget.

Bushra Yasmin Ghazi
5138 Harvard Terrace
Skokie, Illinois 60077

July 1983

CONTENTS

Name _____

THE *KUFFAR* TRY TO KILL RASULULLAH [S]

Find the correct answer.
Color as directed.

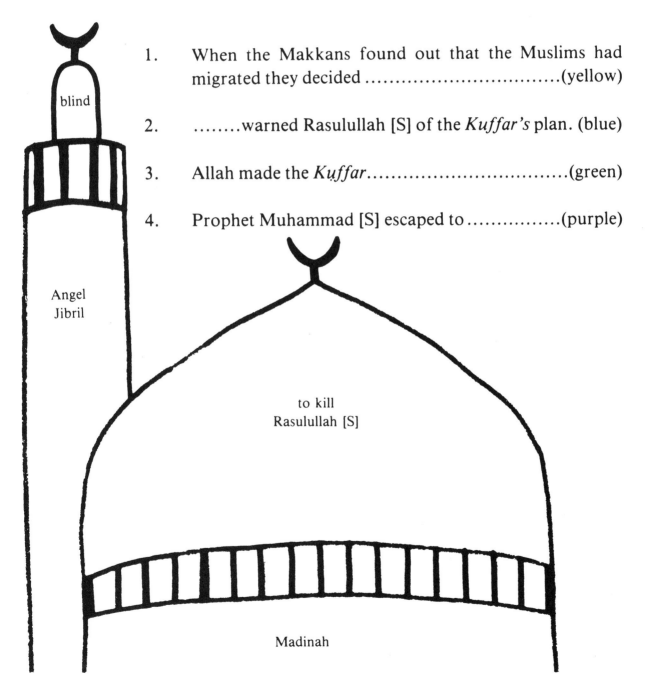

1. When the Makkans found out that the Muslims had migrated they decided ....(yellow)

2. ....warned Rasulullah [S] of the *Kuffar's* plan. (blue)

3. Allah made the *Kuffar*................................(green)

4. Prophet Muhammad [S] escaped to ....(purple)

blind

Angel Jibril

to kill Rasulullah [S]

Madinah

Name_____

RASULULLAH [S] IS WELCOMED
IN MADINAH

1. Draw a line to show the way Rasulullah [S] and his friend Abu Bakr [R] reached Madinah.

2. Color this picture.

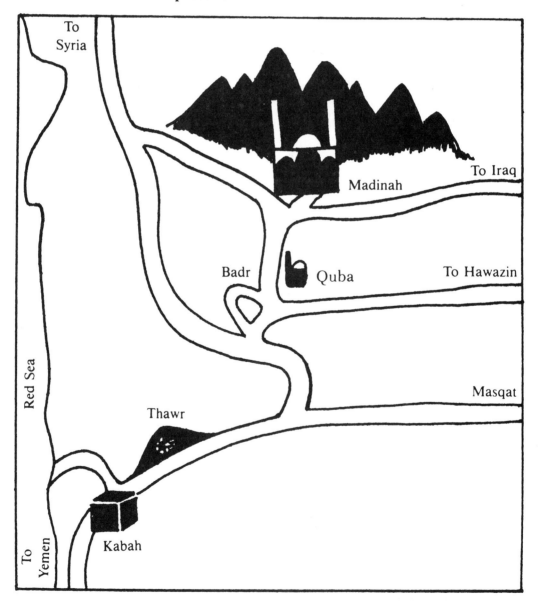

THE *KUFFAR* ARE ANGRY

Find the answers of the following questions in different parts of the tent and color as directed.

1. What city did Prophet Muhammad [S] migrate to?
    Red

2. What did the leaders of the *Kuffar* decide to do?
    Orange

3. Why did the *Kuffar* think that they could win?
    Blue

4. What did Rasulullah [S] become when he arrived in
    Madinah? Green

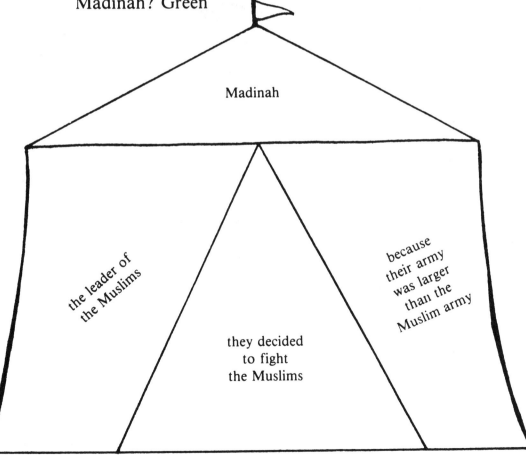

THE BATTLES WITH THE *KUFFAR*

Complete the following sentences by finding the answers in the parachutes and color as directed.

1. The first battle with the *Kuffar* was at .... Red

2. After one year of Badr the *Kuffar* attacked again at ...... Green

3. The *Munafiqun* helped the .... Orange

4. Then one night Allah sent a wind at the..................... Purple

5. The Battle of the Ditch was won by the .... Yellow

6. The Battle of the Ditch went on for......................... Blue

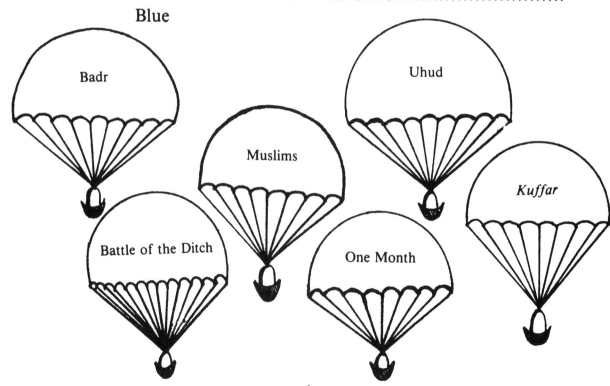

4

Name _____

RASULULLAH [S] WRITES
TO THE KINGS

Color the true petals red. Color the false petals blue.

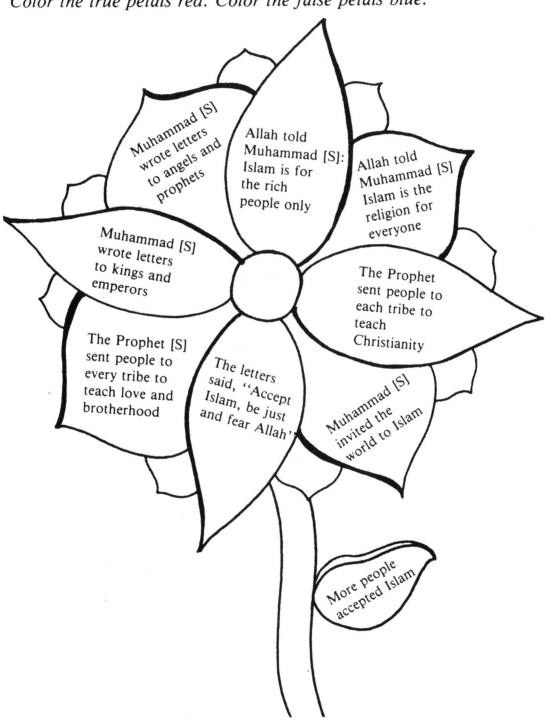

THE KABAH BECOMES THE HOUSE OF ALLAH AGAIN

Help the Muslims get to the Masjid. Select the right word from the "path" below and write it in the blank spaces.

1. The Makkans broke their.............with Rasulullah [S].

2. Prophet Muhammad [S] said, "We will make the Kabah the House of ....once again.

3. A big Muslim army marched towards.......................

4. All Muslims prayed to Allah, "O Allah, give us ....

5. The Muslims captured the leader of the.....................

6. ....forgave the leader of the *Kuffar*.

7. Muslims won Makkah without a ....

8. Rasulullah [S] ....the idols out of Kabah.

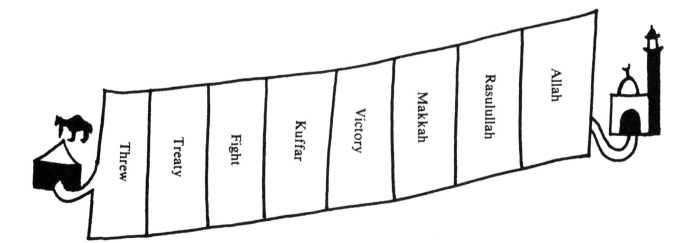

6

RASULULLAH [S] SPEAKS
TO THE MAKKANS

Each leaf belongs to a root.

1. Find the matching leaf and root.
2. Color them the same color.

7

THE MAKKANS ACCEPT ISLAM

Color as directed.

1.   Rasulullah [S] forgave.......................................Red

2.   The *Kuffar* accepted Muhammad [S] as ....Blue

3.   Rasulullah [S] told the Makkans ....Green

4.   Now the Makkans ....in Islam. Yellow

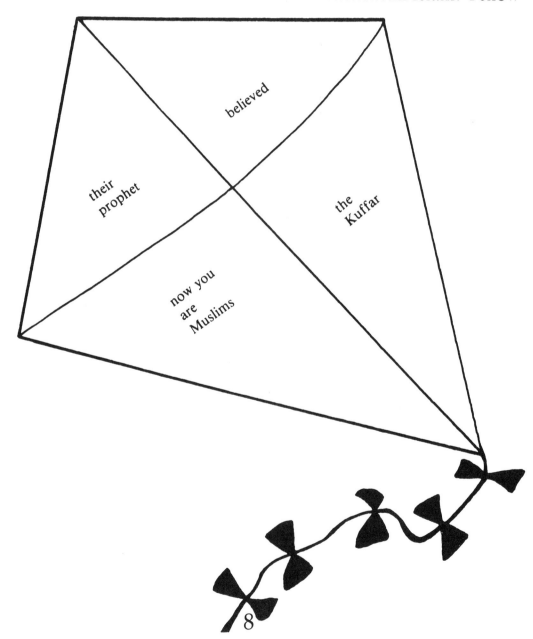

RASULULLAH [S] MAKES HIS LAST HAJJ

Select the correct word and fill in the blanks.

1. More and more people came to ....

   Madinah   Makkah   Washington

2. Allah told Muhammad [S] that his work was..............

   Still incomplete   completed

3. One day Rasulullah [S] decided to go for...................

   A visit   Hajj   A walk

4. Rasulullah [S] stood on a hill in the Valley of ....

   Niles   Utah   Arafat

5. Rasulullah [S] made his ....big speech in the valley.

   First   Second   Last

6. Prophet Muhammad [S] said, ''Remember, all human beings are..''

   Enemies   Brother and Sisters   Strangers

7. Prophet Muhammad [S] asked the people to follow the
   ....

   Idols   Quran   Stars

8. People told the Prophet [S] that they would do whatever ....asked them to do.

   The Prophet [S]   The King   The President

RASULULLAH [S] PASSED AWAY
IN MADINAH

Find the right answer and color as directed.

1. In Madinah Rasulullah [S] became ....Green

2. He asked Abu Bakr [R] to lead......................Black

3. One day he told his wife, Aishah, to give everything he owned to the..Red

4. One day he told his daughter, Fatimah,"............"Blue

5. He said, "Allah is the best ...."Orange

6. He became sicker and soon he.......................Purple

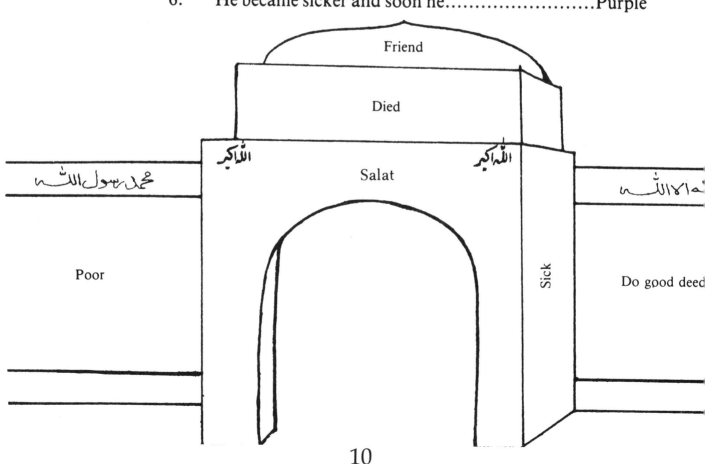

OUR PROPHET:
MUHAMMAD RASULULLAH [S]
HIS WORK GOES ON AND ON

Circle True or False in the following sentences.

T   F   1.   All those who are born will die.

T   F   2.   Muhammad [S] was not a human being.

T   F   3.   The Muslims chose Umar [R] as their leader after Prophet Muhammad's death.

T   F   4.   The leader of the Muslims was now called the *Khalifah.*

T   F   5.   The Muslims chose Abu Bakr [R] as their first *Khalifah.*

T   F   6.   Abu Bakr [R] said, "I will not follow the *Sunnah*".

T   F   7.   The Muslims did not want to work for Islam.

MUSLIMS LOVE MUHAMMAD [S]

Circle the correct answer.

1. Today, there are about.............Muslims in the world.
    One billion   Nine million   Twenty thousand

2. The Muslims are.....................................in Islam.
    Not related   Brothers and Sisters

3. Muslims believe in:
    T   F   a. Allah is One
    T   F   b. Allah's sons
    T   F   c. Allah's angels
    T   F   d. Holy Books
    T   F   e. Many gods
    T   F   f. Allah's prophets
    T   F   g. The Day of Judgement

4. Allah wants us:
    T   F   a. To offer *Salat* 5 times a day
    T   F   b. Not to keep *Sawm* in *Ramadan*
    T   F   c. Not to give *Zakat*
    T   F   d. To make *Hajj* once in our life